If you live HERE

Written & Illustrated By April Diaz de Leon

AuthorHouse™
1663 Liberty Drive
Bloomington, IN 47403
www.authorhouse.com
Phone: 1-800-839-8640

First published by AuthorHouse 10/10/2011

ISBN: 978-1-4634-3007-8 (sc)

Library of Congress Control Number: 2011918324

Printed in the United States of America

Any people depicted in stock imagery provided by Thinkstock are models,
and such images are being used for illustrative purposes only.
Certain stock imagery © Thinkstock.

This book is printed on acid-free paper.

Because of the dynamic nature of the Internet, any web addresses or links contained in this book may have changed
since publication and may no longer be valid. The views expressed in this work are solely those of the author and do not
necessarily reflect the views of the publisher, and the publisher hereby disclaims any responsibility for them.

authorHOUSE®

If you live
HERE

Alpha Phi –
You are the house that gave me a home
and the sisters that gave me a family
during some of my most impressionable years.
thankyou for my favorite memories and
closest friends!

–April Diaz de Leon
University of Missouri
2006-2010

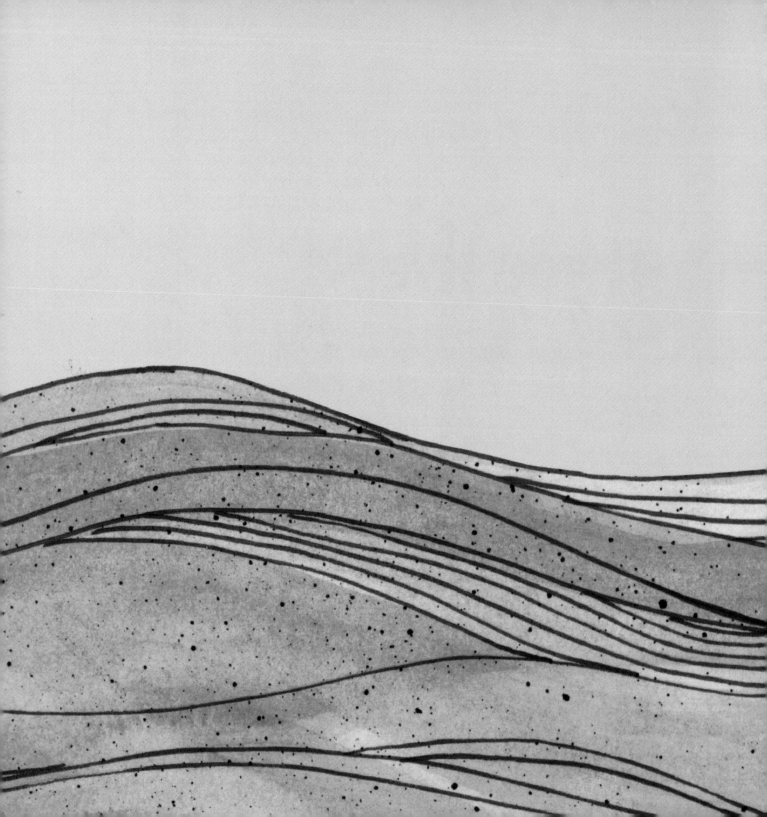

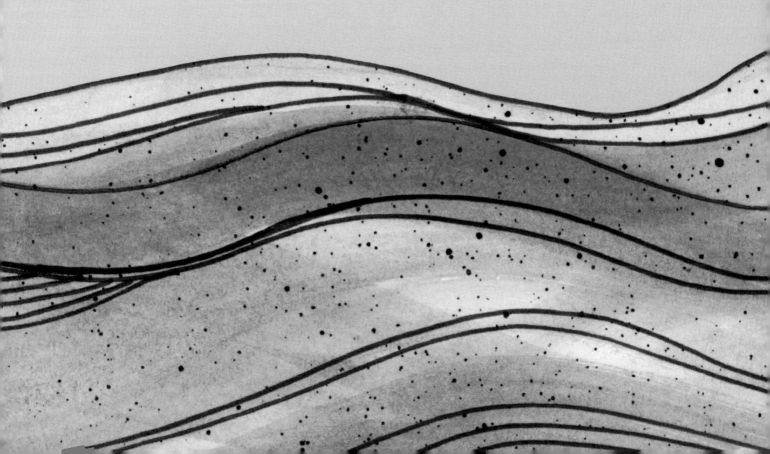

Dedicated to my parents,
Ben and Dana, whose love made our house a home.

If you live
IN A SHELL,

you might be
a turtle.

If you live
IN A HIVE,

you might be a bee.

If you live
IN THE
SKY,

you might be a cloud.

And if you live
IN THE FOREST,

you might be a tree.

If you live in a swamp

You might be a gator.

If you live in this hill,

And if you live in a pot?

you might be
A PLANT!

If you live
in a bakery

you might be a

cake.

If you live in a **spaceship** you might be GREEN.

If you live

IN A GARDEN,

you might be a flower.

And if you live in a shark tank

you might be

mean.

Wherever you live,

Whatever the spot,

be sure to be

GRAT

EFUL

for all that you've got.

A house in **the sky,**

A house in the sea,

A house ain't a HOME

The
END

CPSIA information can be obtained
at www.ICGtesting.com
Printed in the USA
253002LV00001B